CW00429683

ULSTER'S SHIPS & QUAYSIDES

A PHOTOGRAPHIC RECORD

To Margaret

With thanks.

ROBERT ANDERSON
IAN WILSON

Published 2011 by
Colourpoint Books
Colourpoint House, Jubilee Business Park
Jubilee Road, Newtownards, BT23 4YH
Tel: 028 9182 6339
Fax: 028 9182 1900
E-mail: info@colourpoint.co.uk
Web: www.colourpoint.co.uk

First Edition
First Impression

Copyright © Colourpoint Books, 2011
Text © Robert Anderson and Ian Wilson, 2011
Illustrations © Various, as acknowledged in captions

Copyright has been acknowledged to the best of our ability. If there are any
inadvertent errors or omissions, we shall be happy to correct them in any future editions.

All rights reserved. No part of this publication may be reproduced,
stored in a retrieval system or transmitted in any form or by any means, electronic,
mechanical, photocopying, scanning, recording or otherwise, without the prior
written permission of the copyright owners and publisher of this book.

The authors have asserted their right under the Copyright,
Designs and Patents Act, 1988, to be identified as authors of this work.

A catalogue record for this book is available from the British Library.

Designed by April Sky Design, Newtownards
Tel: 028 9182 7195
Web: www.aprilsky.co.uk

Printed by W&G Baird, Antrim

ISBN 978-1-906578-81-7

Explore, discover and buy other titles on Northern Ireland
subjects at BooksNI.com – the online bookshop for Northern Ireland

ULSTER'S SHIPS & QUAYSIDES

A PHOTOGRAPHIC RECORD

Robert Anderson

Ian Wilson

INTRODUCTION

As an island nation we are still dependent on the sea, ships, seamen and our ports for the majority of the province's trade and commerce with Britain, Europe and the rest of the world. Some twenty years ago, in 1990, we collaborated to publish a volume of historical maritime photographs of how those ships, seamen and quaysides of Ulster appeared in pictures taken in the one hundred years or so between the advent of photography in the 1840s to about the end of the Second World War in 1945. Captured in a single volume for the first time were some of the stunning images we had discovered during our researches into Ulster's maritime history. From the great sailing ships and majestic liners of the Victorian and Edwardian eras, many of them the products of a burgeoning shipbuilding industry in the province, to the humble sailing vessels and steam coasters that served the many small ports around our coast at the time, we endeavoured to present an accurate and interesting cross-section of shipping of the period. Included also were impressive views of many of our busy ports and small quays showing just how important they all were to our trade and commerce at a time prior to road transport and of course air travel. The inevitable shipwrecks, groundings and incidents that occurred around the treacherous coasts were also recorded as were some of the colourful characters and more humorous moments of life at sea.

Since that book was published we have become aware that the changes which have occurred between the late 1940s and the present time are equally staggering. As observers of, and participants in the maritime scene in the province, we have again co-operated to present what we hope is an interesting and representative selection of images and text reflecting the major changes that have occurred during the period and which we felt justified in re-visiting. We hope you agree.

Even the casual observer will have noticed the major changes that have taken place in the maritime scene. Ships are larger, faster and generally further away from public view, access to ports is more restricted, containerisation and freight trailers have become the norm and indeed that many of the small ports have declined or become redundant and no longer host commercial shipping. Ports and infrastructure have evolved whilst moving seaward. At Londonderry port facilities have moved several miles downstream to a new facility at Lisahally, Warrenpoint Harbour has been totally redeveloped and the Port of Belfast has not only grown in size but been moved closer to the Irish Sea on reclaimed land. We have witnessed the closure to commercial ships of places such as Letterkenny, Portrush,

Bangor, Dundrum and Newry. Residential apartments have replaced ships at Carrickfergus and Killyleagh whilst trade has declined dramatically at Coleraine, currently the last surviving small port. The fishing ports have seen huge trawlers appear to compete internationally and the harvesting of mussels and other species has seen the introduction of new types of vessels around the coast. New technology in the form of wind turbines and tidal current generators are beginning to impact on our seascape and are even being assembled in the yards and slipways of Harland and Wolff who no longer build ships. Leisure boating and marinas have impacted enormously on Ballycastle, Glenarm, Carrickfergus, Bangor, Ardglass and many of the smaller harbours around the coast.

The growth in air travel has also had an effect on our ports and many people now prefer to make use of abundant and relatively cheap air routes to Britain and the Continent rather than travel by sea thereby removing them from a traditional connection with ships and the sea. Routes to Glasgow, Ardrossan, Liverpool, Heysham Douglas, Oban and Campbeltown were, not very long ago, offered from a variety of Ulster ports. Those of us who prefer sea travel, or those who have no option other than to travel by ship, have become accustomed to crossing the North Channel now in journey times marketed in minutes rather than hours! Large, modern, high speed ships operate on just a few of the traditional routes, some of which are only offered on a seasonal basis.

Gone are the days when men and boys could walk down a quayside to look at the ships, stand at a quayside and watch cargo being unloaded, banter with the dockers or run errands for the crew. This is something the authors can relate to and it forms an important part of our personal memories. In a relatively short space of time, security has become a number one priority followed closely with the obsession for 'health and safety'. The world has become a very different place in a relatively short space of time. Our selection of photographs generally record a connection with ships and the sea and a lifestyle which has gradually disappeared, almost without being noticed by the general public.

The photographs we have used have been selected from a variety of sources including well-known museum collections and little known private collections. The quality of the images do vary of course but have been used purely for their content and interest. Quite a few are appearing in print for the first time and some of the more recent digital images are stunning in their quality and detail. The captions are as factual as possible and are based on information researched by the authors from a great variety of sources. We owe a great debt of gratitude to the many people who had not only the interest but the foresight to record our ever changing maritime heritage and we hope that you will enjoy our selection of evocative images.

Robert Anderson and Ian Wilson
December 2010

CARLINGFORD: THE LAST DAYS OF TRADE

Carlingford is one of the most historic ports in Ulster, in the shadow of the great Norman castle built in the 12th century to control Carlingford Lough. By the 1960s though, it was small and outdated for modern trade. Here is the Dutch coaster *Deo Duce* loading potatoes in April 1966, one of the last two or three such exports. However, latterly vessels engaged in local aquaculture can often be seen in Carlingford. (Ian Wilson Collection)

MUSSEL DREDGER AT ROSTREVOR

New life has also been brought back to Rostrevor quay by aquaculture. On Carlingford Lough, Belfast Lough and Lough Foyle mussel dredgers, are at work, some much larger than the *Celtic Harvester* here, one of the traditional ex-Dutch type. The seeding and harvesting of the mussels beds is a sophisticated, computer-controlled industry. Rostrevor quay was visited by the local Mourne schooners and small steam coasters until the 1930s. (Aubrey Dale)

MAIDEN VOYAGE OF THE *OAK*

Joseph Fisher and Sons of Newry were leading shipowners whose coasters, mostly named after types of wood, were familiar all round the Irish Sea. In 1953, they took delivery of the *Oak* from Messrs. Scott of Bowling on the Clyde. Here she is welcomed in Warrenpoint on her maiden voyage. This tidal basin was the original 18th century harbour, now completely superseded by a modern port. Sold and renamed *Saint Bridget*, the *Oak* met a strange fate in 1972 – deliberately blown up off Land's End when her cargo of explosives became unstable! (Ian Wilson Collection)

SPEED AND POWER ON CARLINGFORD LOUGH

The German-owned container ship *Emma* is typical of the coastal successors of ships like the *Oak* and *Deo Duce*. Carrying a surprisingly small crew, usually of mixed nationalities, and flying flags of convenience, they are built for speed and fast turn-arounds by shoreside gantries. However it is how most of the country's imports and exports, from tyres to televisions to supermarket trolleys, arrive and leave, all done behind high security fences and CCTV. (Aubrey Dale)

THE *OLIVE* OF NEWRY IN THE CANAL

The final ship built for Fishers was the *Olive*, completed by Scott's yard at Bowling in December 1963. Here she makes a fine sight on the historic Newry Ship Canal. Vessels locked in and out at the Victoria Locks a few miles below Newry and made a striking sight sailing just beside the Newry–Omeath road. Although the canal closed to cargo ships in 1974, thankfully the lock gates have been maintained and in recent years Newry has welcomed visiting sailing ships and the excursion vessel *Balmoral*. (Jim Topping)

A BUSY DAY AT THE ALBERT BASIN, NEWRY!

The importance of a small port to the local economy is well conveyed by this bustling scene taken about 1968. The Danish coaster *Finnlith* has brought timber direct from the Baltic while a huge amount of coal has come on three ships, the *Saint William* (in distance, left) and the *Olive*, while the other Fisher collier of the time, *Walnut*, is also just discernible. The crews of Fisher's ships were largely drawn from the area, a tradition with other Ulster shipping companies too, like John Kelly Ltd. and Head Line, that has sadly died out altogether. The dockside here is now the site of the Quays Shopping Centre! (John Matthews)

STEAM COASTER AT KILKEEL

Small steamers like this evolved in the late 19th century to serve hundreds of small harbours and quays all round the Irish Sea. The last of their type, 'single hatch', finished in 1965. The basis of commerce until the coming of the motor lorry in the 1920s was to move goods by water from as close to the point of production as possible, to as close to the market as possible. Thus every few miles along the coast ships were handled, a scene unknown to us today. Rostrevor, Kilkeel, Annalong, Newcastle and Dundrum, only 20 miles apart, imported coal and exported potatoes and Mourne granite. The name of this ship is unknown. (Robert Anderson Collection)

SINGLE-HATCH STEAMER *FIRST* IN ARDGLASS

No-one is in sight as the *First* lies aground at low tide in the 1950s. This shows the strength of construction needed for these vessels, as they regularly took the ground at the smaller ports. Their cargo of 300 or 400 tons was a day's work with the ship's gear, the crew having to go to work, maybe after a rough passage. But they would then walk to the pub, or call at a nearby farm for fresh milk and eggs. The *First* together with (inevitably!) the *Second* and *Third* belonged to Isaac Stewart of Belfast and was the last ship built at Maryport in Cumberland, in 1906, under the name *Admiral*. (Ian Wilson Collection)

CASTLE BAY SETS OUT TO FISH

In spring sunshine, the *Castle Bay* departs from Kilkeel in 1985. When she was built for Richard Donnan in 1965, she was one of the biggest vessels in the Northern Irish fleet at 75 feet (22 metres) and 100 gross tons. She ventured as far as Shetland for herring and also caught prawns and whitefish. Decommissioned in 1995, she was hauled ashore at Annalong as an exhibit for the Annalong Development Association, but like all too many preservation schemes, it stalled and the boat was broken up in 2007. (Ian Wilson)

THE *CORAL STRAND*, A CLASSIC CO. DOWN BOAT

The 57 foot *Coral Strand* was typical of hundreds of boats fishing out of Portavogie, Ardglass and Kilkeel from the 1950s onwards. Some are still to be seen. She was built at Arbroath in 1966 and went into service as a herring ring-netter, partnered by the *True Token*. Her owner was James Palmer of Portavogie. In the 1970s she was sold to Kilkeel, where she is seen here the same day as the *Castle Bay*, and was decommissioned in 1994/5. The hard-working crew were accommodated in a surprisingly snug fo'c'stle cabin. (Ian Wilson)

NEWCASTLE: FIRST SHIP FOR 19 YEARS!

On 14 June 1971, the small Norwegian coaster *Gullfjord* was piloted into Newcastle harbour, and began unloading her cargo of empty barrels. Kilkeel harbour was closed for engineering works and Annalong had a tricky entrance, so the ship was sent to Dundrum, but a Danish ship was on the berth, unloading timber, so she sailed across the bay to Newcastle, which had seemingly closed forever to coasters in 1952. The *Gullfjord*, which is still trading today, is a modern successor to the single-hatch steamers, but the busy Norwegian coastal trade still needs such vessels, as road transport is difficult. (Ian Wilson Collection)

IN THE SHADOW OF SLIEVE DONARD

The mate of the *Gullfjord* operates the cargo winch as a local team discharge the barrels, destined for the new Kilhorne Seafoods factory, Annalong. Left to right are John Bartlett, Haydn Chambers and John McClelland. Compared with the steam winch and the wooden boards that covered the old steamers' hatches, the work aboard was less back-breaking in these new diesel ships. Several more foreign coasters used Newcastle for this trade over the next two years. (*Mourne Observer*)

BALTIC TIMBER ARRIVES IN DUNDRUM

Dundrum, reached through a tricky, sandy channel, was an important port serving the area's needs. The East Downshire Steamship Company owned the harbour and operated several colliers and a large sailing ship in the 1890s, the *Ruby*, which imported timber direct from Canada. Until the late 1970s, timber was still unloaded, and here the Danish *Lonni* is seen on 14 June 1971, the same day the *Gullfjord* was diverted to Newcastle. The last ship called at Dundrum in 1985, the Manx *Ben Veen*. Note the Norman castle on the hill. (*Mourne Observer*)

LOW TIDE, DUNDRUM, OCTOBER 1967

Dundrum port had a railway connection, a siding from the main Belfast –Newcastle line of the Belfast and County Down Railway, running down the quays. The derelict railway warehouse of 1869 can be seen here. In a lowered and generally unrecognisable state, it is now private dwellings, while housing has also spread all over the old harbour, just like at Killyleagh. The small *Yarvic* belonged to Nicholas Anley of Kilkeel, but efforts to run her profitably on the Irish Sea were doomed to failure. On occasions, she sailed with a gallant crew of two! (Ian Wilson)

FAREWELL TO STEAM IN ULSTER!

Although it is very difficult to be positive, this steam dredger may well have been the last coal-fired steamship to work in a local port, after a story that goes back to 20 April 1816 and the arrival of the *Greenock* in Belfast, the first steamer to cross from Scotland to Ireland. This is the dredger *Mannin 2* engaged in maintaining depths at Kilkeel in April 1978. There was an attempt to preserve her as a historic steamship, but like the *Castle Bay* and too many others, it failed and she sank at Weston Point on the Manchester Ship Canal in 2003. (Ian Wilson)

LONDONDERRY HARBOUR COMMISSIONERS' PORT DREDGER

A similar steam vessel the *Aberfoyle* is seen here at Ardglass in June 1967. The *Aberfoyle* was a Dutch-built dredger which from time to time undertook contracts outside her home port. This is still the case with her modern counterpart, the *Lough Foyle*, which has done a lot of work at Drogheda, Workington and the new Stena ferry port near Cairn Ryan. Another unusual assignment for the *Aberfoyle* was to convey a road-surfacing machine from Ballycastle to Rathlin Island in 1965. (Ian Wilson)

BREAKING THE IRISH CEMENT STRIKE (i)

Ardglass, an important medieval port, experienced its busiest scenes in modern times in 1970. The Irish construction industry faced ruin because of a cement-workers' strike. Out of the way ports on both sides of the border were used to import cement from all over the U.K., and on one day seven coasters were in at once. Here we see the Dutch *Emerald Trader* which has arrived from Boston in Lincolnshire on 21 June. A Danish ship lies astern of her. (Jim Topping)

BREAKING THE IRISH CEMENT STRIKE (ii)

The Ardglass trade would have been the last time a traditional Scottish 'puffer' ventured across to Co. Down. This is the *Eldesa* which ran with cement from Portpatrick to Ardglass, on one occasion putting into Bangor for shelter. She is the classic 66 foot type (developed to navigate the locks in the Forth and Clyde Canal). The *Eldesa* earned the distinction of being the final such ship to trade, as she was modernised and renamed *Eilean Eisdeal,* continuing until 1994. She can now be visited at the maritime museum, Inveraray, Loch Fyne. (Ian Wilson Collection)

QUITE AN EVENT AT ARDGLASS!

When the Russian refrigerated vessel *Pskovityanka* commanded by Captain Grashchenkov arrived on 17 December 1995, she became the largest vessel to call, being 60 metres in length and of 1058 gross tons. She took on 391 tons of frozen mackerel for Saint Petersburg, which must have been a valuable cargo as it was worthwhile her coming all the way from Saint Petersburg to load it. She returned for more early in 1996.
(J.O. Smyth)

LARGE CO. CORK TRAWLER IN ARDGLASS

Although registered in Skibbereen, the *Sea Spray* belongs to Castletownbere. In the summers of 2009 and 2010 she and others from Castletownbere have fished for herring in the Irish Sea and landed at Ardglass. A couple have also sheltered in Bangor. At 43 metres, they are a huge advance on the typical Co. Down boats exemplified by the *Castle Bay* and *Coral Strand* but they are really midwater pelagic boats and not typical of boats normally landing in Ardglass. The other traditional Co. Down fishing harbours, Kilkeel, Annalong and Portavogie, could not handle their size. (Aubrey Dale)

CLARENDON DOCK, BELFAST: THE *INDORITA* DEPARTS

Taken on 6 April 1966, this view is entirely different today. Only the Rotterdam Bar (built in 1797) remains as a reminder of 'Sailortown' among the urban renewal. Clarendon Dock dates from 1870 but the drydock leading off it is much older and therefore preserved today, thankfully. The little *Indorita*, an old ship dating from 1920, has discharged bagged flour from Birkenhead, the last commodity handled here. Even if the tight modern regulations could be met, the economics of running a small ship like this on the Irish Sea now are impossible. (Ian Wilson)

STRANGFORD QUAY: THE *ISLE OF LEWIS* DEPARTS

Strangford is another historic place, listed in 1281 as one of the 'five ports of Ulster'. But by the 1950s, poor road access and the increasing size of ships were seeing these small ports cease trading one by one. Strangford's coal imports continued till the early 1980s. On a quiet day around 1964, the *Isle of Lewis* is casting off after unloading coal. She belonged to the Hebridean Cunningham family who also over the years had the *Isle of Harris*, *Glas Island*, *Isle of Rona* and *Eilean Glas*, all familiar in Ulster harbours. (Ian Wilson Collection)

SALVAGE STEAMER AT PORTAFERRY, 1952

It is a wet day with no-one about as a plane flies over Portaferry and a photographer captures the salvage steamer *Black Knight* alongside the quay. She has been working on the Lamport and Holt liner *Lassell* which ran aground on the South Rock off Cloughey. One of the open motor boats used on the ferry service to Strangford can be seen opposite the Portaferry Hotel. The *Black Knight* was a former Grimsby trawler dating from 1918. (M.A. Meadowcroft)

THE POWER OF THE SEA: KEARNEY, 1962

In March 1962, a southerly gale blew this ship, the Dutch *Frida Blokzijl*, helplessly north after leaving Dundalk. Cloughey lifeboat under Coxswain Walter Semple gallantly took off Captain Jan Blokzijl and the crew of four, before the ship was deposited on the jagged rocks at Kearney. Coxswain Semple was later decorated for the rescue. The *Frida Blokzijl* was eventually refloated and towed to Portaferry, but did not sail again. She had escaped from the German occupation of the Netherlands in 1940. (Robert Anderson Collection)

DONAGHADEE HARBOUR IN THE EARLY 1950s

Donaghadee has a fine harbour dating from 1834. Sir John Rennie the eminent engineer designed it, and it was constructed of the best Anglesey granite, to be an improved Irish terminal of the short sea route for mail, passengers and livestock from Scotland. Superseded by Larne to Stranraer in the 1870s, Donaghadee continued to import coal and other cargoes. Here a coaster typical of the smaller ones operated by John Kelly Ltd. of Belfast slowly approaches her berth, the *Ballyarnot* ex- *Tamnamore*. Kellys renamed all their ships *Bally-* in 1951–52. (Ian Wilson Collection)

DONAGHADEE HARBOUR: THIRTY YEARS LATER

Not much has changed, but then happily it never does in Donaghadee harbour, which amazingly still features one of the two original hand-cranes installed in the 1830s! Here the Coleraine Harbour Commissioners' grab dredger *Bar Maid* (cleverly named because of the troublesome sand bar at the mouth of the River Bann) is undertaking a contract to dredge Donaghadee harbour. In 2010, with the *Bar Maid* long sold, the work was tackled by the *Lough Foyle*, a suction dredger which was one of the largest ships ever to enter Donaghadee harbour. (Robert Anderson)

A VIOLENT GALE, BANGOR BAY

The hazards of trading to small harbours is illustrated by the plight of Kelly's *Ballyclare*, caught in a northerly gale at the Central Pier, Bangor, in February 1957. Every few years this would happen, as the harbour had no shelter from the north, and sometimes the ship would be deliberately driven on to the flat sand between this and the South Pier. An unsuccessful attempt was made to construct a breakwater across the Bay about 1815, but is was not until the North Breakwater (now the Eisenhower Pier) was built in the late 1980s was the problem largely solved. By then, though, commercial shipping had finished. (Ian Wilson Collection)

A CALMER DAY, BANGOR

Coal discharge is proceeding normally in this view dating from about 1972. The ship is the *Saint Colman* belonging to J. and A. Gardner of Glasgow, who carried most of Bangor's coal in this era. She was built with the lock gate dimensions at Newry in mind, and was named after the town's Patron Saint. The lorries seen here rumbled through the town traffic, and with hoteliers also complaining about coal dust from the pier, times were changing for a traditional import. The last coal cargo came in 1987, and now no-one would know where their coal is from - it could be Vietnam, Columbia, South Africa or elsewhere! (Ian Wilson Collection)

A SCHOONER RETURNS TO HER BIRTHPLACE (i)

The *Result* was one of the finest sailing ships of her day, constructed by Paul Rodgers of Carrickfergus in 1893 and famous all round the British Isles coast. She had a long life (latterly aided by an engine) and traded until laid up in Exeter in 1969. In 1970, she was acquired by the Ulster Folk and Transport Museum and sailed under veteran skipper Tom Jewell for Carrickfergus via Brixham and Dun Laoghaire. She arrived in Belfast Lough on 18 November and here mate Percy Lamey (another old West Country seafarer, formerly skipper of the *Bessie Ellen*) meets the Belfast pilot boat which brought out, among others, George Thompson the Museum Director and shipping enthusiast Don Patterson. (Don Patterson)

A SCHOONER RETURNS TO HER BIRTHPLACE (ii)

The graceful lines of the *Result* are evident in this view from near the bows. Apparently, discussion on her design was so prolonged that someone asked 'What will be the result of all this?' and so the name was conceived! After arriving at Carrickfergus, the *Result* moved to Belfast while discussions (even more prolonged) continued about her future. Eventually, in 1979 she was transported by road to the Museum site and has sat there ever since. Some ship-lovers feel that if the Museum, although well-intentioned, had not bought her she could well be sailing yet – her true purpose. (Don Patterson)

The old steam tug *Southampton* served her owners, Messrs. Cooper, who did most of the towage at Belfast, for many years until the mid-1960s. Here her crew are depicted, about 1950. Captain Bartlett is on the extreme right, Jack Mahood is second from the left and third from left is a man named Ennis, from Carrowdore in North Down. (Bob Mahood)

BUILDING THE *BEATRICE O'NEILL*

This fine fishing boat was built by Arthur Clapham at his now-forgotten Glen Boatyard, near Bangor in 1946. It was at the foot of Strickland's Glen and during the war built lifeboats and assorted barges, etc. for naval use. The *Beatrice O'Neill* fished out of Annalong, but sank off the Cumberland coast in 1949. Third from the left is the youngest of the workforce, Hal Patton. Best known for the 'Glen' class yachts, Arthur Clapham later moved his operation to White Rock in Strangford Lough. (Ian Wilson Collection)

THE HEAD LINE STEAMER *BENGORE HEAD*

The Ulster Steamship Co., principals G. Heyn and Sons Ltd. but familiarly known
as Head Line, were Ulster's foremost operators of deep-sea ships for over a century
from 1877. Gustavus Heyn, having come to Belfast as Consul for Prussia, married
and settled in County Down. The firm was most associated with their trade to
Canada and into the Great Lakes, but their smaller freighters such as this also had
a thriving connection with Baltic ports. The *Bengore Head* had been captured as
the *Kalliope* in the Allied advance through Germany and served the Head Line till
1967, by which time this type of steamship was rapidly going out of date as diesel
container ships took over. (World Ship Society)

THE LAST HEAD LINE FREIGHTER

When the *Inishowen Head* was completed at Sunderland in 1965, the days of the traditional freighter were numbered. Cargo carried securely in containers, which could be swiftly lifted on and off by one man in a crane instead of a gang of dockers, were the future. She would have been one of the last of her type. In 1970, the drastic step was taken to remove all her masts and derricks and convert her into a container ship. Sold in 1979, she only lasted three more years before being broken up in Korea. (World Ship Society)

OVERNIGHT TO GLASGOW

The traditional overnight Belfast–Glasgow route of Burns and Laird Lines made a huge step forward with the arrival of the fine diesel pair *Royal Ulsterman* and *Royal Scotsman* in 1937. They both had a distinguished war record on trooping and other duties, as far away as Madagascar in the case of the *Ulsterman*. By 1967, car ferries were becoming the norm, and the economics of ships like these lying all day at Belfast or Glasgow rather than the more rapid turn-around of new ferries rendered them obsolete. The overnight service to the heart of Glasgow thus ended after nearly 150 years. (Ian Wilson Collection)

OVERNIGHT TO HEYSHAM

Each night in the 1950s passenger vessels (a ferry was something that only crossed a river!) left Donegall Quay for Glasgow, Heysham and Liverpool. The *Duke of Lancaster* was one of a trio introduced in 1956 and 57 which made the crossing to the railway port of Heysham in Lancashire in just over seven hours, with a train connection to Euston arriving at 11.35 a.m. The increase in air travel, the 'Troubles' and the evolution of car ferries combined to finish this route in the mid-1970s. The *Duke of Lancaster* became a static tourist and shopping attraction in the Dee estuary, Cheshire. (Ian Wilson Collection)

SUMMER IN THE 50s: the ISLE OF MAN STEAMER

This impressive view is looking back towards the Queen's Bridge as the daylight Isle of Man steamer *Mona's Queen* departs with holiday-makers. Before package holidays to the sun, the island was enormously popular with Ulster families. The ship could call at the very long pier at Ramsey and disembark passengers for the hotels there, before sailing on to Douglas. The post-war class of fast, graceful steamers such as this, the *Snaefell*, *King Orry* and others made a fine sight racing up or down Belfast Lough on a summer's day. Unsuccessful efforts have been made to preserve the last of them, the *Manxman*. (Ian Wilson Collection)

ON THE OTHER SIDE OF THE LAGAN

In the previous view, the coal barges and cranes at the Queen's Quay can be discerned. Here is a close-up scene of the heart of Belfast's vital coal trade. The city was the only industrial city in the U.K. without coal nearby. John Kelly Ltd. were the foremost coal importers, one of their main customers being Belfast gasworks. The barges were towed by the company's small tugs under the Queen's and Albert Bridges to the gasworks quay until the 1960s. The *Ballykesh* was one of a class of eight colliers built by Lewis of Aberdeen in the mid-1930s, and was built as the *Baronscourt*. (Ian Wilson Collection)

THE *BALLYHALBERT* IN ABERCORN BASIN, BELFAST

The *Ballyhalbert* had formerly been the *Coleraine* before Kelly's renaming policy. This scene is just behind the present giant Odyssey building and is very different today, although the basin is still used from time to time by visiting sailing ships. It was a hub of noisy, grimy commerce with coal imports, scrap exports and the Hamilton drydock, in which a ship can be seen in the distance. In sanitising such elements of a port's history for 'heritage' purposes, however, (in this case 'Titanic Quarter') the essential authenticity and character is lost. (Ian Wilson Collection)

THE *LOCH ETIVE* IN ABERCORN BASIN

John Rainey of Larne, trading sometimes as Rainey Enterprises, owned several coasters including the *Loch Linnhe* and *Kathar* and was the first local owner of the passenger boat *Maid of Antrim,* which he brought from the Clyde in 1966. The *Loch Etive* is seen here in his colours in or around 1964. She had a steam engine despite being built for London owners in 1948, when Dutch and German diesel coasters were starting to dominate the European coastal trades. This is no doubt why her career under the Red Ensign only lasted till 1968. Kellys were also very conservative and ordered new steam colliers into the mid-1950s. (Ian Wilson Collection)

SAINT COLUM 1

This ship operated the overnight Belfast to Liverpool service from Donegall Quay for a number of years following the establishment of Belfast Car Ferries Ltd. in 1981. The company took over a long established route that had been terminated by P&O the previous year. Senior Master of the vessel was the popular Captain Fullerton of County Down, who regularly took his ship through the narrow channel between the Copeland Islands and the Co. Down coast sounding the ship's siren as he did so, much to the delight of passengers and locals alike. New, much larger and popular vessels are now operated on the route by Norfolk Line. (Robert Anderson)

FERRY GOOD IDEA

A scheme to provide a fast passenger ferry connection linking Bangor, Carrickfergus and Belfast almost became a reality in 2001 when two new, state of the art, fast passenger craft were delivered to Belfast from Australia. Regular 30 minute passages to the towns were planned to arrive at and depart from Donegall Quay. Financial and planning difficulties eventually forced the abandonment of the scheme and the fast craft were transported by sea to Nigeria for operations there before returning to the Thames where they now operate successfully. *Antrim Runner* is seen proceeding down Belfast Lough for onward shipment to Nigeria. (Robert Anderson)

INNOVATIVE DESIGN

The impressive *Stena Voyager*, looking like something out of a science fiction movie, makes her way slowly to her berth in Belfast following a high-speed crossing from Stranraer in Scotland. Stena Line introduced these huge innovative vessels on several of their routes in the UK to offer fast crossings and quick turn-round times. A record turn-round of under 30 minutes was achieved by this vessel in Belfast. Mooring is accomplished extremely quickly using automated hydraulic systems, so no ropes are needed, and the cavernous car deck can be cleared and reloaded via a linkspan in minutes. These ships are not cheap to run though.
(Aubrey Dale)

QUEEN'S QUAY 2010

A major dredging scheme commenced on the River Lagan upstream of the Port of Belfast in September 2010. Spoil dredged further upstream was transferred from barges onto the 1964 built grab hopper dredger *Hebble Sand*, berthed at Queen's Quay, for disposal at sea. The well-kept 870 ton vessel is seen arriving at the start of the 6 month contract. The visible changes to the quaysides in this re-vamped area of the city are immediately apparent when comparisons are made with earlier photos. (Aubrey Dale)

STEAM SHIP AND CRANE AT DONAGHADEE

The pleasantly-named *Snow Queen* is captured by an early user of colour film at Donaghadee in the early 1950s. She belonged to Howden Brothers of Larne. The steam crane had, until the line's closure in 1950, unloaded some of the cargoes into wagons of the Belfast and County Down Railway for onward transport to Newtownards or Comber. The railway had extended down the harbour in the first place to convey passengers to the very side of the steamer taking them to Portpatrick, and its tracks are still visible today. (Ian Wilson Collection)

LUXURY COMES TO BANGOR BAY

The superb Cunard Line *Caronia* anchored in Bangor Bay most summers between 1954 and 1966. She usually came from Oban and sailed for Dun Laoghaire on her British Isles itinerary. In those days, only the very rich went on cruises, and it was automatically assumed by the awe-struck locals that the Americans coming ashore were millionaires! The millionaires were usually greeted on Bangor pier by Irish dancers (unless it was an Ulster Sunday!). The *Caronia* would be surrounded by curious onlookers in small yachts and boats, one of whom has taken this terrific photograph. (Ian Wilson Collection)

FAREWELL TO THE *HELEN CRAIG*

After an extraordinary 68 years service to one owner under the same name, the *Helen Craig* sets off from the Queen's Quay for the breaker's yard in 1959. The important but forgotten 'other' Belfast shipyard, Workman Clark, built her in 1891 and she was employed firstly carrying coal, but later became a regular sight at her berth just below the Queen's Bridge, on a regular run to and from Preston with general cargo. Her owners were Hugh Craig and Co. Ltd, who had started in the 1860s with sailing colliers like the *Indian Queen* and latterly became part of the Cawood group. (Robert Anderson Collection)

FAREWELL TO THE *CRAIGOLIVE*

Another Craig coal-burner leaves the Lagan for the breaker's. This time it is the *Craigolive* and the year is 1965. She had been built at Barnstaple in Devon in 1921 along with a sister *M.J. Craig* and so gave sterling service over 44 years. However the age of steam was rapidly ending and expensive repairs to these ships were not worth undertaking. Later the same year, Belfast's last coal-burning coaster the *Craigantlet* was also scrapped. (Robert Anderson Collection)

THE FAMOUS *CANBERRA* TAKES SHAPE

The P&O liner *Canberra* is one of the most famous ships Harland and Wolff ever built, although it has always been said the firm lost a huge amount of money on the contract, which was completed in 1961.Nevertheless, the great white ship earned fame not just as very popular cruise liner but as troopship, quickly pressed into service in the Falklands conflict of 1982. The *Canberra* as her name suggests, though, was initially intended for a regular service from the U.K. to Australia via the Suez Canal, but the increase in air travel ended this leisurely mode of travel. (William Holden)

AN EARLY OIL RIG: *SEA QUEST*

The futuristic profile of the *Sea Quest* took shape to great public interest at Harland and Wolff, being completed in 1966. She was a very early example of a purpose-built semi-submersible oil rig. The *Sea Quest* earned a place in the history books in 1970 when she discovered for B.P. the Forties Field in the North Sea, the first commercially viable find in the U.K. sector. By 1979 it was producing 25 % of the UK's oil needs. In January 1980, *Sea Quest* had a blow-out and fire off the coast of Nigeria which led to her having to be scuttled in deep water. (William Holden)

BUNCRANA PIER

Few photos exist of commercial shipping at Buncrana Pier in Lough Swilly. This interesting view of the Dutch coaster *Avanti* was taken in June 1964 as the ship was discharging a cargo of bagged fertilizer. It is believed that the ship had a small fire in the cargo and had put in here to have it extinguished. An assorted collection of modes of transport await loading along the quayside. (Robert Anderson Collection)

BALLYMONEY COMES TO LARNE

Many pictures exist of Kelly ships at various ports in Northern Ireland but this beautiful colour shot of the *Ballymoney* berthed at Larne begged inclusion. The ship is seen alongside one of the main harbour berths and may be waiting to move around to the coal berth at Bank Quay. Larne Harbour has seen almost continual and major development as a ferry port since this photo was taken in September 1969. *Ballymoney* stayed in the Kelly fleet from new in 1953 until she was scrapped in 1971. (Ian Wilson Collection)

THE LAGANSIDE QUAYS, 1980

For 150 years, the Co. Down bank of the Lagan was used for coal and other bulk cargo, and the Co. Antrim side for passenger and livestock traffic across the Irish Sea. However now this scene, taken from the Queen's Bridge is unrecognisable, with new road and rail bridges, the clearing away of the coal depots and the scrap berth, at which the Dutch *Daniel* is loading, and the moving of the passenger terminals downstream. A side-effect of this is that the port is moved out of sight of the average person, and divorced from general consciousness in a way that our forebears would have found odd, especially on an island! (Ian Wilson)

PADDLE STEAMER *WAVERLEY*, DONAGHADEE, 1991

The famous *Waverley* is the last sea-going paddle steamer in the world. Her main season is spent in the Firth of Clyde, but in the last thirty years she has visited most parts of the British Isles. There was great excitement in Donaghadee in 1991 when she put in twice, once, seen here, for an excursion to the Isle of Man and then a few days later for a one-way trip to Warrenpoint. As Donaghadee harbour was built for paddle steamers of the 1830s, it was historically significant to welcome the last of her type although much longer! (Ian Wilson)

RATHLIN RELIEF

During *Canna*'s annual dry docking a relief vessel was normally provided by the operators of the Rathlin service, Caledonian MacBrayne. The *Raasay* was one of a small class of similar vessels operated by the company around the Western Isles of Scotland and several of the class provided relief cover over the years. A new operator on the Rathlin service has chartered *Canna* to continue to provide a service for vehicles and has added a new, passenger only, high speed vessel to improve the links with the island. (Aubrey Dale)

LAY-UP BERTH

During the winter months the P&O fast catamaran *Express* is usually at her lay-up berth at Donegall Quay, seen here in evening sunlight. The 91 metre, 6000 ton vessel is based at Larne during the season. Other than small craft this is about as close to a large ship that people crossing the River Lagan now get. This quay was once the hub for passenger services to Ardrossan, Liverpool and Heysham and many photos exist of the quay lined with vessels. A paddle steamer service to and from Bangor also operated from here in the first half of the 20th century. (Aubrey Dale)

SAGA ROSE IN BANGOR BAY, 2009

This magnificent ship was one of the last 'classic' ocean liners when she was built in 1965 as the *Sagafjord* at Toulon for the Norwegian America Line. By 2009 though, when this picture was taken, time was catching up with her and new international safety rules due in 2010 meant it was her last season. Cruise liners, happily, are being welcomed to Belfast in increasing numbers, and some also anchor off Bangor just like the *Caronia* in the 1950s and 60s. The elegant *Saga Rose*, to general regret, was scrapped in China in 2010. (Ian Wilson Collection)

QUEEN VICTORIA

This superb view of the Cunard cruise liner *Queen Victoria* was taken in 2010 as the ship sailed out of Belfast following a visit that was part of her 'Round Britain' cruise programme. Easily the largest of the cruise ships now occasionally making Belfast a port of call, she is one of a growing number of such vessels that can be seen at locations around the Ulster coast during the summer months. The cruise market has seen phenomenal growth over recent years and is no longer seen as 'elitist'. Many recent newbuildings can accommodate up to 4000 passengers and crew and even larger ships are planned for the future. (Aubrey Dale)

FERRIES AT LARNE

This impressive photograph illustrates two of the modern P&O ferries currently operating out of Larne Harbour. The Japanese built, 21,000 ton, car and passenger vessel *European Highlander* is just departing on her normal run to Cairnryan and her fleetmate *European Mariner* is loading commercial trailers at another berth. The *Highlander* is one of two near sister ships built specifically for the Larne to Cairnryan route between 2000 and 2002. They can each carry 410 cars. (Aubrey Dale)

COLERAINE AT BELFAST

The 212 gross ton tug *Coleraine* was built for Cory Ship Towage (NI) Ltd. in 1970 and served in their fleet based at Belfast for almost 40 years. The Cory tugs based here provided services at Belfast, Londonderry and for incidents in the North Channel and Irish Sea. They were part of a large organisation operating tugs all around the UK and Irish coast. Despite being named after the Ulster port town the vessel never actually visited Coleraine due to her deep draft. The vessel recently relocated from Belfast to another UK port. (Sean McCafferty)

A PAIR OF GIANTS

Seen together at Harland & Wolff's fitting out berths at Belfast in August
1978 are two of the largest ships ever built in the UK. Ordered in 1976
the 333,000 deadweight tonne super tankers *Coastal Hercules* and her
identical sister ship *Coastal Corpus Christi* were built for the USA based
Maritime Fruit Carriers group. Both were eventually handed over to their
owners by the shipyard in March 1980 following costly and protracted
discussion regarding payment for the ships. Harland & Wolff completed
30 more ships before building ceased in 2003. (Robert Anderson)

LAST SLIPWAY LAUNCH

The final slipway launch from Harland & Wolff took place on 25th September 1980 when the 7100 ton Sealink car and passenger ferry *Saint David* went down the ways at Queen's Island. The ship was one of four almost identical sister ships ordered by the company. She was named by a presenter from the BBC Television's popular children's programme 'Blue Peter'. After service on routes to Wales the ship returned to Northern Ireland to run alongside her sister *Galloway Princess* and was eventually renamed *Stena Caledonia*. She still operates on the popular route to Stranraer today. (Robert Anderson)

The Milewater Basin at Belfast was formerly home to the RNR Headquarters ship *HMS Caroline*, a veteran of the Battle of Jutland. She is seen here with the 'Ham' class inshore minesweeper *HMS Thatcham* and 'Ton' class minesweeper *HMS Laleston* alongside. Both of the smaller ships were attached to the Belfast RNR. *HMS Caroline* remains in use at Belfast, at another berth, with an uncertain future at the time of writing. (Robert Anderson)

S.S. DIVIS

Divis was a sludge disposal vessel which sailed daily to dumping grounds off the Copeland Islands at the mouth of Belfast Lough. She is seen here in Milewater Basin at the end of her long career in 1982 awaiting decisions on her fate. Belfast built by the Workman Clark yard in 1928 she was eventually scrapped, only her engine being removed for preservation by the Ulster Folk and Transport Museum. (Robert Anderson)

CARRICKFERGUS

This dramatic view of Carrickfergus Harbour during a south westerly gale was taken in the 1950s. Spray from waves crashing against the harbour wall almost obscures the crane which continues to discharge the steam coaster, believed to be *Downshire*, alongside the quay. The photograph illustrates the narrowness of the harbour entrance. Railway tracks run along the quay towards the town, just a short distance away. The area has, like many former port areas in the province, changed almost beyond recognition with reclamation having taken place. Roads, apartments, retail outlets and a marina now occupying the area seen here to the right of the pier. (Sean Neeson Collection)

CLYDE VALLEY

The harbour at Carrickfergus played host to this old vessel for a number of years in the early 1970s. *Clyde Valley* had been involved in gun-running to Ulster during troubled times in Ireland in 1914 which led to the formation of the UVF. The ship was discovered in Canada in 1968 and funds were raised to return her to Northern Ireland with a view to restoring the ship. Like many such schemes the practical and financial implications proved too much. The ship was eventually towed away from the port and broken up at Lancaster in 1974. (Sean Neeson Collection)

UNDER TOW

The Belfast owned sludge disposal ship *St. Stephen* is seen here being moved off her lay-up berth in Carrickfergus harbour by tugs of the McLoughlin fleet prior to being taken over by Mediterranean owners. The vessel had been engaged in dumping at sea from Belfast but this practice was outlawed by new European regulations. The McLoughlin tugs are operated around Belfast Lough and at Larne Harbour by a long established local family firm which continues to add new vessels to its fleet. *(Sean Neeson Collection)*

BANK QUAY

Close to Curran Point within Larne Lough and just next to the main road between Larne and Carrickfergus is the coal discharging berth which was operated by the local firm of Howdens. This long established company were ship owners at a time and were later absorbed into the John Kelly group. The quay was used by ships of the Kelly fleet delivering coal to the area and occasionally by other vessels delivering limestone chippings to a nearby limeworks. A narrow and shallow channel led to the berth from the main shipping channel in Larne Lough and the quay is now disused. Kelly's 1300 ton motor vessel *Ballylesson* is seen alongside in the early 1980s. (Robert Anderson)

ENTRANCE TO LARNE

Larne Harbour has become one of the busiest ferry ports in the UK. Several of the main ferry companies operate sailings from here to ports in Scotland and England on what is the shortest direct route to the mainland. Large modern ferries, high speed craft, tankers, cargo ships, cruise ships and tugs can all be seen passing through the entrance to Larne Lough. P&O's *Express*, which operates a seasonal fast service to Troon and Cairnryan, is pictured entering the harbour in the summer of 2009. (Aubrey Dale)

ACCIDENTS DO HAPPEN

This embarrassing accident to the Townsend Thoresen ferry *Ionic Ferry* occurred in March 1987 as the vessel was swinging in fog to berth stern first at her ramp. The stern of the ship grounded just out of the channel at the entrance to the port. The locally based McLoughlin tug *Samuel F.* was called to assist but as she had grounded on a falling tide the ferry had to wait for the next high tide to be refloated. No serious damage was done to the ship and she remained at Larne for several years following Townsend's takeover by P&O. (Robert Anderson)

ROLL-ON / ROLL-OFF

Pioneering roll-on / roll-off freight and passenger services to Preston were operated from Larne Harbour by vessels of the Atlantic Steam Navigation Company. The *Baltic Ferry*, seen here at Larne in June 1970, began life in 1945 as a tank landing craft with the US Navy. The company operated several similar ex-LSTs in the role prior to dedicated new tonnage being built. The impact of these types of ships appearing on North Channel routes to England and Scotland can not be overstated and indeed shipping in Ulster would never be the same. (Sean Neeson Collection)

POWER STATION JETTY

The storage tanks at Ballylumford Power Station were supplied with oil delivered by large tankers to the jetty within Larne Harbour. Fairly typical of the type of tankers to visit here is the Liberian registered *Maria Venizelos* photographed in 1971. The tankers were piloted to this berth by Belfast Pilots who used Belfast Harbour based tugs to assist berthing and departure. (Maxwell Blair)

CRUISE SHIP

Larne is just one of several ports in Ulster to benefit from the recent boom in British Isles cruising holidays. In recent years cruise liners have also called at Killybegs, Londonderry, Portrush, Ballycastle, Rathlin, Belfast and Bangor. The Portuguese flagged *Athena* is seen here being assisted by the Belfast based tug *Willowgarth* as she swings around in Larne Lough. Passengers can be seen on deck enjoying the pleasant evening summer sun. (Aubrey Dale)

MAGHERAMORNE JETTY

This jetty, at the southern end of Larne Lough and requiring a local pilot for ships using it, served a cement manufacturing plant. Public access was not permitted but a reasonable vantage point has been found by the photographer here. This 1969 photo shows the Kelly ship *Ballyhaft* alongside, probably delivering a cargo of coal to be used in the cement making process. The factory operated two small dredgers which worked within the lough dredging clay which was also used in the process. One of them can be seen at the small jetty in the foreground. (Maxwell Blair)

CIVIL WORKS

The ex-Admiralty TID type tug *Somerton* is pictured in June 1948, at work at the southern end of Larne Lough, assisting in the laying of power cables across the lough from Islandmagee. She was one of a large batch of such tugs built around the UK during the Second World War specifically for naval dockyard use. *Somerton* was owned after the war by Belfast Harbour Commissioners and was engaged in a variety of tasks over the years. (Sean Neeson Collection)

IRISH LIGHTS TENDER

The Irish Lights tender *Isolda* is framed by the vessels *Commodore Goodwill* and *Bardic Ferry* as she manoeuvres just off the berths at Larne Harbour in this 1965 photograph. Buoys and lighthouses which provide mariners with vital navigational information around the entire Irish coast have always been maintained by Irish Lights. Seen in the background here are the tall chimneys and the jetty of the old coal-fired Ballylumford Power Station, since replaced by a modern oil and gas fired generating plant. (Maxwell Blair)

GLENARM

Two small 'puffers' lie moored to the pier at Glenarm on a calm and sunny day in April 1966. These small cargo ships are waiting to load the products of the limestone quarry seen in the background. This raw material was used in the steel-making industry that existed then in Scotland. The ships are *Lady Isle*, dating from the 1940s, and *Raylight* dating from 1963. Both vessels were familiar visitors to many of the smaller Ulster ports. *Raylight* was lost on the Maidens off Larne in dense fog in May 1975, fortunately without loss of life. (Sean Neeson Collection)

GLEN SHIEL AT GLENARM

The small, modern motor ship *Glen Shiel* is photographed loading limestone from a lorry at Glenarm harbour about 1970. This handy little 195 ton ship was built in 1959 to serve the communities on the Scottish islands and was one of the large fleet operated by the well known 'puffer' management company Glenlight Shipping of Glasgow. Several small companies had merged to form Glenlight. *Glen Shiel* was just 109 feet long with a beam of 24 feet. She sank off the Scottish port of Ayr in June 1973. (Sean Neeson Collection)

'PUFFER' HARBOUR

Often seen in the harbours along the Antrim Coast north of Larne, loading limestone or discharging coal, small cargo ships collectively known as 'puffers' were a familiar sight. The name derived from the sound made by the exhaust of the original single cylinder steam-powered vessels and remained in use even after the vessels converted to diesel engines. The small harbour at the village of Carnlough was one of the places these ships were loaded regularly. The Glasgow registered *Moonlight* is seen here loading bags of limestone via chutes whilst another vessel opposite awaits loading. (© National Museums Northern Ireland collection, Ulster Folk and Transport Museum)

WARLIGHT

The obsolete 1932 lines of the 200 ton motor ship *Warlight* are evident in this 1960s view of the ship moored at the entrance to Carnlough harbour. The inner berths are occupied and the vessel is waiting its turn to load. *Warlight* was another member of the former Ross & Marshall Company whose vessels all ended with the suffix 'light'. They and the Hay Hamilton owned vessels, which were prefixed 'Glen', were later branded as Glenlight Shipping. (Maxwell Blair)

ANTRIM COAST INCIDENT

On her way through the North Channel in February 1963 with a cargo of potatoes from Londonderry the Dutch ship *Zevenbergen* somehow managed to go aground, in the middle of the night, on the Antrim Coast near the village of Carnlough. Although not seriously damaged, and in no real danger from the settled weather, the ship remained aground for a few days. It took the might of a large and powerful naval salvage tug summoned from the Clyde to drag the ship away from the shore. This photo shows interested locals observing the activities to refloat the ship. (Ian Wilson Collection)

Situated on the scenic coastline of the Glens of Antrim the pier at Red Bay has been in existence for well over a century. Shown here alongside the outer end of the pier, during one of her cruises from Campbeltown in Scotland, is the historic paddle steamer *Waverley*. The ship is the last of her type and as well as operating cruises on the Clyde is seen at various locations around the coast during the summer months. Her trips to Red Bay have always been well patronised by Scottish and local residents alike. (Ian Wilson)

BALLYCASTLE

Harbour facilities at Ballycastle had remained relatively unchanged for decades. Ferries from Rathlin Island had to endure an exposed berth to land and load passengers, animals and freight. The island ferry *Iona Isle*, a converted fishing boat and one of two vessels operating the service, is seen here in 1983 loading building blocks for the island. Her operator was the late Tommy Cecil, an islander who campaigned for years to have the harbours improved. (Maxwell Blair)

BALLYCASTLE IMPROVEMENTS

During 1996 the very basic harbour facilities at Ballycastle were significantly improved to accommodate a cross channel link to Scotland, the Rathlin ferry service and provide a sheltered marina. A huge quantity of stone to build breakwaters was imported from Norway for the project. This photo illustrates the Rathlin car ferry *Canna* loading vehicles for the island, the Campbeltown ferry *Claymore* and the dredger *Bar Maid* together in port in 1997. (Robert Anderson)

RATHLIN HARBOUR

The 736 gross ton coastal cruise ship *Balmoral* operates short public cruises from a great number of UK ports throughout the summer months. She arrived at Rathlin Harbour for the first time in August 1992 during a visit to the province and is seen here alongside the Manor House pier. The ship has made frequent visits over the years to various ports around the Ulster coast. Built in 1949, originally for service in the Bristol Channel, the ship is now operated by Waverley Excursions Ltd. (Tommy Cecil)

HIGHLAND CONNECTIONS

For a few seasons in the late 1970s a high-speed, foot passenger only ferry operated crossings from Portrush to Oban in an attempt to reinstate historical links between the town and Scotland. Seen arriving at Portrush for an earlier trial run is the Norwegian built catamaran *Highland Seabird*. With a crossing time of about 4 hours the service was poorly used and, despite adding a 'Duty Free' attraction by calling at Moville in the Republic of Ireland during its last season, failed to attract sufficient customers to survive. (Robert Anderson)

PUFFER RESCUE

People gather to watch the arrival of the motor 'puffers' *Pibroch* and *Dawnlight 1* at Portrush in August 1975. The *Pibroch* was summoned to tow the *Dawnlight 1* into port following an engine failure when she was on passage from Portrush to the Western Isles with a cargo of blocks. Both ships were managed by the same company thus avoiding expensive towage charges. *Pibroch* currently lies rusting away in the west of Ireland. (Robert Anderson)

AIR SEA RESCUE LAUNCH

This fine view of the RAF Air Sea Rescue launch 2757 at speed off the County Antrim coast was taken by the former commanding officer of the unit based at Portrush. No. 1105 Marine Craft Unit moved there from the Foyle in 1963 and remained until 1971. They originally operated two of this type and two smaller units. A large craft, *Seal*, was a later addition. This vessel is preserved at the entrance to the Royal Air Force Museum at Hendon in London. (Robert Anderson Collection)

ELEVATED VIEW

The British coaster *Fallowfield*, berthed in Portrush, is viewed here from the jib of a container crane in 1968. She operated a short-lived container service to Preston from here alongside her sister ship *Fernfield* and the *Wirral Coast*. On her deck can be seen bundles of pit-props and trailer flats, and on the quayside RAF technicians examine a recently arrived engine destined for one of the high speed Air-Sea Rescue craft based in the harbour at that time. (Robert Anderson Collection)

DREDGING

The Londonderry Port and Harbour Commissioners steam dredger *Aberfoyle* at work in Portrush Harbour in June 1963. At the time the RAF Air Sea Rescue launches based in the Foyle were about to be relocated to Portrush. This small dredger served many of the smaller ports around the coast at that time and was eventually scrapped in 1975. In the background are the stone bins which held a total of 500 tons of local basalt quarry stone ready for shipping to the mainland and Europe. (Robert Anderson Collection)

PORTRUSH QUAYSIDE

A unique photograph of Portrush Harbour taken in early March 1964 shows the coasters *Silverthorn* and *Wirral Coast* in the small harbour with the minesweeper *HMS Wiston* alongside. *Silverthorn* is loading a cargo of stone from the concrete bins, *Wirral Coast* is discharging containers and the warship had called to drop off an Admiral who lived locally. The harbour was closed to commercial shipping in the early 1990s but is still home to a busy Severn class lifeboat. (Hugh McGrattan)

ROYAL VISIT

In her Silver Jubilee year of 1977 Queen Elizabeth visited Northern Ireland on board the Royal Yacht *Britannia*. As Her Majesty was due to hold a reception at the University of Ulster in Coleraine, the Royal Yacht arrived off Portrush and the Queen was transferred by Royal Barge to the accompanying destroyer *HMS Fife*. From the warship's small flight deck the Queen and her party were flown by helicopters of the Queen's Flight the short distance to Coleraine. *Britannia* is being watched over in this view by the minesweeper *HMS Gavinton* and the smaller *HMS Thatcham*. (Robert Anderson Collection)

STEAMER'S FAREWELL

The last steamship operated by S.W. Coe was the *Banntrader*. This 1920 built veteran became part of the Coe fleet in 1950 and ran regularly to Coleraine until 1963. Newly built motorships had replaced the steamers. She is seen here leaving Portstewart Bay for the last time on her way to the scrapyard in Holland having just dropped off her pilot. The steam whistle is sounding her final salute. (Robert Anderson Collection)

CASTLEROCK CASUALTY

In February 1981 the Panamanian registered vessel *Burgundia* was outward bound from Coleraine with a cargo of seed potatoes destined for Portugal. Atlantic swell at the Barmouth caused the ship to bottom on the sand bar at the river entrance and caused damage to the rudder and propeller. As a result the vessel went ashore on Castlerock beach where

AGROUND

The Dutch vessel *Bern* is seen here high and dry in the River Bann having gone aground in fog whilst proceeding upriver to Coleraine to load potatoes in November 1964. The pilot had not seen a channel marker and the ship was too far to starboard. Most of the river bed is mud and sand so the vessel was refloated with no damage at the next high tide and was able to continue her voyage. The channel to Coleraine from the sea is just over 5 miles in length. (Robert Anderson)

CRAMMED QUAYS

The bridge over the River Bann at Coleraine provided an excellent vantage point for photographing shipping in the port. This 1955 view shows the steamships *Bannquest*, *Lascar*, *Magrix* and *Bannqueen* alongside the quay with other ships out of sight in the background. The 'Bann' ships were regular traders to the port with coal and general cargo and were owned by the Liverpool firm of S.W. Coe. The little 'puffer' *Lascar* was on a weekly general cargo service between Londonderry and Coleraine for the Laird Line. (Robert Anderson Collection)

NEW BERTH

Over 150 men were registered as dockers at Coleraine Harbour during the 1950s. Many of them are seen here involved in the discharge of loose Scandinavian timber from the Dutch coaster *Dora* in September 1954. The ship was the first vessel to use a newly constructed concrete berth at the busy port. Some 500 ships a year used the riverside facilities here during the mid-1950s delivering coal, general cargo and timber and exporting potatoes and pit-props. This was the busiest time on record for the town centre port. (Robert Anderson Collection)

RUSSIAN TIMBER

The first modern cargo of Russian timber arrived at Coleraine in October 1958 aboard the German coaster *Erich Haslinger* and is seen being unloaded by a large number of dockers. The cargo was made up of loose planks that had to be handled and assembled into 'heaves' before being lifted ashore by the ship's own derricks to be wheeled away on bogies to waiting lorries. In the background harbour cranes unload coal and load pit-props. This area is now a town centre car park. (Robert Anderson Collection)

Working as a docker usually involved some heavy manual labour. This is well illustrated in this scene of dockers at Coleraine discharging large sacks of animal feed from one of S.W. Coe's steamers. The photograph was taken in 1954 at what was known as the 'Liverpool berth' close to the Bann Bridge. Weekly sailings between Liverpool and Coleraine were operated by the company. The term 'general cargo' could include the one-hundredweight bags seen loaded on the hand truck. Some of the men are not in their youth! (Robert Anderson Collection)

ACTIVE QUAYSIDE

This unusual view of a busy quay at Coleraine Harbour was taken about 1959. Piles of pit-props destined for Welsh mines await export on the quay as cranes discharge coal from the fairly new motorship *Silverthorn*. An older companion from the fleet of S.W. Coe, the steamship *Bannspur*, awaits discharge and the ship from which the photo was taken, the *Bannrose* is securing lines having just arrived. Ahead of *Silverthorn* another motorship is almost hidden in a cloud of steam issuing from the single steam crane still in use. (Robert Anderson Collection)

AWAITING WEATHER TO SAIL

A spell of bad weather and dangerous conditions at the Barmouth, the
entrance to the River Bann, caused delays to ships waiting to sail from
Coleraine in February 1964. Six vessels are seen in this photo of which five
have discharged their cargo and one is loaded with potatoes for export.
S.W. Coe's fleet of motorships, *Blackthorn*, *Maythorn* and *Silverthorn* are
seen here, as is the Dutch ship *Fem* and the British coaster *Isle of Lewis*.
In the background is the small Dutch tanker *Cornelis Broere* and hidden
from view is the German *Elli Ahrens*. (Robert Anderson Collection)

INCREDIBLE EVENTS

In early 1981 an almost unbelievable sequence of events occurred within sight of each other on the north coast. Within the space of a few weeks no less than three ships had become victims of a series of incredible happenings. The Panamanian registered ship *Burgundia* had gone aground on Castlerock beach when outward bound from Coleraine with a cargo of potatoes, the British collier *Nellie M* was boarded and sunk by an I.R.A. gang at Moville in Lough Foyle and the Danish coaster *Erria* had run aground at Inishowen Head after her propeller had been damaged by a drifting log. Of these ships only *Nellie M* was returned to service, the others eventually being scrapped. (Robert Anderson)

RIVER CRUISING

The inland waterways of Northern Ireland are less well-known than those of GB but awareness is growing amongst pleasure boat owners. The *Maid of Antrim* has been based on Lough Neagh since the mid-1960s but has often offered cruises on the 48 mile stretch of the River Bann between the lough and Coleraine. She is pictured here departing from the Cutts just outside Coleraine on her 6 hour return journey to Antrim which involves 4 lock passages en-route. (Robert Anderson)

SAND DREDGING

Well away from public view on Lough Neagh an important activity has been carried on for generations. The dredging of sharp freshwater sand for the construction industry involves several companies and around a dozen or so vessels based at a variety of sites around the largest lake in the British Isles. The vessels involved in the work have mostly been adapted for the role although a few have been specially built. This photo shows the former Dutch river barge *Libertas* discharging sand at the rather basic facilities at Derryclone. (Aubrey Dale)

CARRICKARORY PIER

For decades the pier at Carrickarory, close to Moville at the mouth of Lough Foyle, was used as the base for Foyle Pilots guiding ships in and out of Londonderry. The pier was also used regularly by local merchants to discharge imported coal from small coasters. The Glasgow owned *Saint Brandan* is photographed here in 1970. A pilot cutter, fishing boats and a yacht lie alongside. Foyle Pilots are now based in nearby Greencastle Harbour and fishing boats still use this pier. (Maxwell Blair)

The Royal Navy frigate *HMS Londonderry* is shadowed by an Admiralty tug as she cautiously approaches a berth in the city she was named for. The Royal Navy has had strong connections with the city following the important role it played as a base during the Battle of the Atlantic in the Second World War. Warships of many nations frequently visit the port. *HMS Londonderry* was a 'Rothesay Class' anti-submarine frigate of 2200 tons. She is seen here with her Wasp helicopter displayed on her small flight deck. The ship also visited Portrush many years later just before she paid off in 1984. (Pat Crowley)

FOYLE STEAMERS

Quays along the banks of the Foyle at Londonderry have played host to many types of ships over the years. This view dates from August 1975 and shows the steam dredger *Aberfoyle*, steam hopper barge *Foyle Channel* and the RFA depot ship *Rame Head*. The port's steam-powered dredging fleet at the time also included the *Foyle Clearway*. This part of the city's quays was later substantially redeveloped and was known as Meadowbank Quay prior to the port's move some miles downstream to a newly developed deep water facility at Lisahally. (Robert Anderson)

CITY QUAYS

This 1950s view of the quayside at Londonderry includes a ship from each of the best known Belfast shipowners at the time. In the centre of the picture, and sitting high in the water, is the Head Line's *Torr Head*, having probably discharged grain from the USA. Astern is a ship of the large fleet of John Kelly, possibly *Ballykelly*, discharging coal. It was not uncommon to see ships from both of these companies in Ulster's larger ports during the 1950s and 1960s. (Ian Wilson Collection)

OTHER CITY BERTHS

This downstream view from almost the same location as the previous photograph illustrates just how busy Derry Quay could be. Seen in this late 1950s view are the steam coaster *Monksville*, the *Ulster Weaver* and *Loch Etive* at what were known as 15, 16 and 17 Berths. All three ships were well known in the Irish Sea at the time and *Monksville* was actually the last steamship to visit Coleraine in 1963. (Ian Wilson Collection)

SWINGING IN THE FOYLE

The Russian freighter *Primorsk* is seen here turning in mid-stream in the River Foyle at Londonderry in the 1960s assisted by the Admiralty tug *Empire Fred*. Freighters of this size were once a common sight at the city quays and Russian ships visited frequently. The tug was one of several based here, primarily to assist the visiting naval ships and submarines which participated in exercises in the North Atlantic but which also attended merchant ships when required. *HMS Sea Eagle* was the shore establishment in Londonderry that organised and co-ordinated the exercises and the depot ship *HMS Stalker* was based here. (Robert Anderson Collection)

DEPARTURE FROM DERRY

Seen here departing from Londonderry in 1962 is Kelly's 842 ton *Ballyhaft*.
The ship had been built at Greenock for the fleet in 1952 but in 1955 was
transferred to John Milligen & Co. for several years and is seen here with
their funnel colours. In 1955 the ship came back into the Kelly fleet and
in 1963 was lengthened which increased her tonnage to 991. The vessel
continued in service with the Kelly fleet until scrapped in Belgium in
1970. (Ian Wilson Collection)

QUAYSIDE ACCESS

The Belfast registered *Kathar*, owned by John Rainey of Larne is seen alongside the city quays at the Port of Londonderry in 1967. At this time the main port areas were within sight and sound of the city centre and the general public could actually see ships at close quarters. Derry had regular connections with many other ports in the UK at this time including a passenger service to Glasgow and an early container service to Preston. (Maxwell Blair)

PORTSALON PIER

This pier lies on the western shore of Lough Swilly close to the Atlantic Ocean and was seldom used by cargo ships. This rare photograph shows the small Dutch coaster *Catherina W.* alongside during the late 1950s. The hatches are open and the derricks raised giving the impression that the ship is ready to discharge cargo. On the quay wall can be seen two large buckets of the type used at many small ports to discharge coal into lorries. (John Baird Collection)

APPROACHING LETTERKENNY

Ships trading to Letterkenny in Co. Donegal had a tidal approach to the town along Lough Swilly and the shallow River Swilly to the quayside there. Seen here on one of the bends in the river on the approach to the town in the 1960s is the small Danish vessel *Susanne Jors*. She is being assisted by a small boat just out of shot whilst being watched by a couple of interested locals. It was not uncommon for ships to go aground on the soft mud and have to await the next tide to complete their journey. (John Baird Collection)

LETTERKENNY QUAY

These days it is hard to imagine an ocean going vessel in such a location. This is the quayside at Letterkenny as it was in August 1965. Discharging coal at the small quay is the 330 ton Dutch coaster *Zwartewater*, which dated from 1940. This entire area is barely recognisable today such have been the changes to the landscape. Imports at the port included timber, general cargo and coal. The small area that the ships were turned in when outward bound is seen on the right. The occupants of a Morris Minor car observe the discharge from a safe distance. (Ian Wilson Collection)

MILFORD JETTY

Milford Jetty lies at the head of navigation of Mulroy Bay. Pictured here delivering a cargo of flour to the adjacent mill and bakery in the 1980s is the *City*, of the well-known London based shipping company F.T. Everard. The jetty was built by Lord Leitrim in the 1880s to serve his steamships sailing between ports in the north and north west of Ireland and Britain. Ships delivering cargoes here usually arrived during high spring tides due to the difficulties of navigating the tortuous channel. Pilots for the passage to the pier were usually picked up and dropped off at Rathmullan in nearby Lough Swilly. The small ships of the Everard fleet often loaded stone as a return cargo to the Thames at Coleraine. No commercial ships now use this jetty. (Robert Anderson)

TORY ISLAND

Situated several miles off the Donegal coast is the small inhabited island of Tory. Residents and visitors to the island are served by a regular ferry from Bunbeg on the mainland. During recent harbour improvement works another Donegal based ferry was also used to take material to the island. Seen here at Tory is Aranmore Ferries ex Caledonian MacBrayne ship *Rhum*, one of a class of small car and passenger ferries built originally in the 1970s to service the smaller Scottish islands. The *Canna*, currently serving Rathlin Island from Ballycastle, is another one of the class. (Malcolm Townsley)

KILLYBEGS FLEET

Stringent EU fisheries quotas mean that many trawlers are limited to a certain number of days at sea and are allowed to catch only a certain amount of fish. A result of these regulations is that large numbers of modern and expensive vessels can be seen laid-up and idle in many of the country's fishing ports. This general view of the fishing berths at Killybegs Harbour illustrates just such a scene. The natural harbour here has been a long established fishing port but in recent times has had additional berths constructed to handle not only the largest of the fishing fleet but also oil exploration vessels and cruise ships. (Malcolm Townsley)

MODERN TRAWLER

Like cargo ships and passenger ferries the increase in the size of trawlers
in recent times has been staggering. Having to spend longer at sea, and
going greater distances in search of fish, has resulted in owners investing
in the building of huge modern ships. The Donegal registered *Western
Endeavour* is seen arriving at her home port of Killybegs and is just one of
a new breed of ships that not only catch fish but process them on board in
preparation for landing directly to the market ashore. Ships such as this
can be seen laid up in Killybegs for long periods due to EU catch quota
regulations. (Sean McCafferty)

DONEGAL TOWN

The town quay at Donegal plays host to the small Danish coaster *Birgitte Pedersen* delivering a cargo of timber from the Baltic during the 1960s. With the advent of larger vessels many of the smaller harbours on the Donegal coast and elsewhere saw a gradual decline in the numbers of commercial ships arriving. No ships call here now but the quayside still plays host to pleasure craft, local fishing boats and tourist vessels. (Don Patterson Collection)

MAP OF LOCATIONS

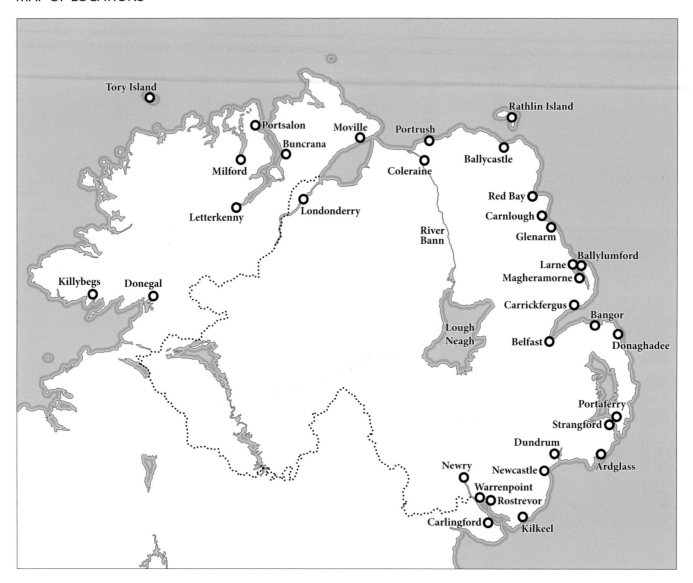

Notes about the Authors

Robert Anderson is an active shipmaster and a Coleraine Harbour Commissioner. He was a River Bann pilot and Dredging Master for almost 30 years and has written several successful books relating to the history of his home town of Coleraine.

Ian Wilson is the Manager of North Down Museum. A former teacher at Coleraine Inst. he is a recognised and respected authority on shipwrecks and has written and broadcast widely on a variety of maritime matters. He still lives in Bangor, the town of his birth.

Acknowledgements

As well as all the photographers who are acknowledged, the authors would like to record sincere thanks to the following for assistance with information or tracing photographs: Ken Abraham (Newry Museum), Terence Bowman ('Mourne Observer'), Jayne Clarke (Mid-Antrim Museums Service), Mark Kennedy, Commander Gilbert Mayes, National Museums Northern Ireland, Don Patterson, Crawford Phin and Malcolm Townsley.

Front Cover:

THE *KING GEORGE V* ARRIVING AT BANGOR, MAY 1970

Expectant Scottish passengers line the decks of MacBrayne's elegant turbine steamer as she approaches Bangor on a unique excursion from Ayr. This was the only time the ship crossed to Ireland, spending most of her long career (from 1926 to 1974) on the world-famous excursion from Fort William and Oban to Staffa (for Fingal's Cave) and Iona. She had been chartered by the Coastal Cruising Association and Mr. W. Paul Clegg. The *King George V* came alongside the North Pier and then Bangor passengers embarked on a cruise towards Portpatrick in Scotland, returning through Donaghadee Sound. MacBrayne's smartly uniformed staff were serving traditional High Tea as the splendid ship pulled away to return to Ayr after a day that recalled the stylish era of sea travel! (William Holden)

ALSO AVAILABLE FROM COLOURPOINT BOOKS – www.colourpoint.co.uk

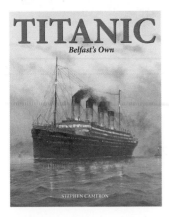

TITANIC - Belfast's Own

Stephen Cameron

Tells the story of RMS Titanic from inception through to disaster and the tragic human connections.

978 1 906578 77 0   £12

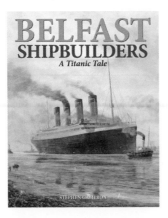

BELFAST SHIPBUILDERS – A Titanic Tale *Stephen Cameron*

Belfast's world famous shipbuilding industry documented via the stories of the families that made it happen.

ISBN 978 1 906578 78 7   £16

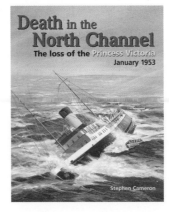

DEATH IN THE NORTH CHANNEL
Loss of the Princess Victoria
January 1953 *Stephen Cameron*

Detailed and sensitive account of a tragic maritime disaster in the waters off N. Ireland.

978 1 904242 01 7   £12

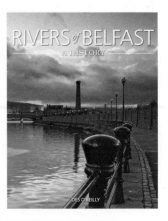

RIVERS OF BELFAST

Des O'Reilly

A celebration of Belfast's rivers brought to life through lavish illustrations, photos and maps.

978 1 906578 75 6   £20

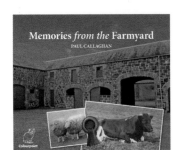

MEMORIES FROM THE FARMYARD

Paul Callaghan

Fascinating and entertaining accounts of the work of notable Ulster farmers and breeders.

978 1 906578 63 3   £8.99

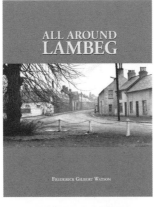

ALL AROUND LAMBEG

Fredrick Gilbert Watson

History of the Lambeg area, its industry and its families. Based on twelve descriptive walks.

978 1 906578 15 2   £25

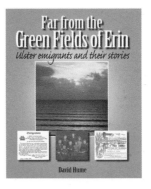

FAR FROM THE GREEN FIELDS OF ERIN

David Hume

Reflection on the many who emigrated from Ulster and their stories and successes.

978 1 904242 42 0   £14.99

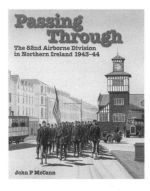

PASSING THROUGH – The 82nd Airborne Division in Northern Ireland 1943-44

John McCann

Story of the Division in Europe and their time training for D-Day in Northern Ireland.

978 1 904242 41 3   £14